I0625502

Mindfulness

Unlock the Power of Presence and Achieve Inner Peace with the Ultimate Guide to Mindfulness: A Transformative Journey to Enhance Your Well-Being, Boost Your Happiness and Live in the Moment

Lance P. Richards

Mindfulness: Unlock the Power of Presence and Achieve Inner Peace with the Ultimate Guide to Mindfulness: A Transformative Journey to Enhance Your Well-Being, Boost Your Happiness and Live in the Moment

Table of Contents

01: Introduction to Mindfulness

Mindfulness is a mental state of awareness and attention that has been gaining popularity in recent years as a powerful tool for personal growth, well-being, and stress management. Mindfulness is the act of bringing one's attention to the present moment, with an attitude of openness, curiosity, and non-judgment. This ancient practice, which has its roots in Buddhism, has been found to be highly effective in helping people overcome stress, anxiety, and depression, as well as promoting physical health, emotional intelligence, and creativity.

The practice of mindfulness is simple, but not always easy. It requires a deliberate effort to focus on the present moment and to cultivate a state of calm and awareness, despite the distractions and pressures of daily life. The benefits of mindfulness, however, are well worth the effort. People who practice mindfulness regularly report a greater sense of happiness, fulfillment, and inner peace, as well as improved relationships, increased productivity, and enhanced overall well-being.

At its core, mindfulness is about cultivating a heightened sense of awareness and presence in the present moment.

01: INTRODUCTION TO MINDFULNESS

This involves paying attention to our thoughts, feelings, and physical sensations, and learning to observe them without judgment or distraction. Mindfulness also involves developing a sense of kindness and compassion towards ourselves and others, as well as cultivating a sense of curiosity and openness to new experiences.

One of the key benefits of mindfulness is its ability to reduce stress and anxiety. In today's fast-paced, high-pressure world, many people struggle with feelings of overwhelm, anxiety, and stress. However, by practicing mindfulness, we can train our brains to be more resilient to these negative feelings and cultivate a state of inner peace and calm. This can have a profound impact on our mental and physical health, and can help us to feel more centered and balanced, even in the face of life's challenges.

Another important aspect of mindfulness is its impact on our relationships. By cultivating a greater sense of empathy and understanding, we can build stronger and more meaningful connections with the people in our lives. Mindfulness also helps us to communicate more effectively and to listen more deeply to others, which can lead to deeper, more authentic connections.

Finally, mindfulness can have a positive impact on our careers and our overall sense of purpose and fulfillment. By helping us to stay focused and centered, mindfulness can increase our productivity and creativity, and help us to be more effective in our work and more fulfilled in our personal lives.

In conclusion, mindfulness is a powerful tool for personal growth and well-being that can have a profound impact on our mental and physical health, our relationships, and our careers. Whether you're looking to reduce stress and anxiety, build stronger relationships, or achieve greater fulfillment in your personal and professional life, mindfulness can help you to unlock the power of presence and achieve inner peace.

02: The Science of Mindfulness

In recent years, the practice of mindfulness has received increasing attention from the scientific community. Researchers have been studying the effects of mindfulness on the brain and the body, and have discovered a wealth of evidence supporting the many benefits of this ancient practice.

One of the key areas of research in the science of mindfulness is the impact of mindfulness on the brain. Studies have shown that regular mindfulness practice can lead to changes in brain structure and function, including increased thickness in regions associated with attention and sensory processing, and increased activity in areas associated with positive emotions and self-control.

In addition to its impact on the brain, mindfulness has also been found to have a positive impact on physical health. Studies have shown that mindfulness can lower blood pressure, improve immune function, and reduce pain and inflammation. Additionally, mindfulness has been found to be an effective tool for managing chronic health conditions such as heart disease, cancer, and chronic pain.

Mindfulness has also been found to be highly effective in managing stress and anxiety. By training the brain to be more resilient to stress and negative emotions, mindfulness can help to reduce symptoms of anxiety and depression, and improve overall emotional well-being. Additionally, mindfulness has been found to be an effective tool for managing symptoms of post-traumatic stress disorder (PTSD) and other mental health conditions.

Another area of research in the science of mindfulness is its impact on cognitive function. Studies have shown that mindfulness can improve attention, working memory, and executive function, making it an effective tool for improving overall cognitive performance. Additionally, mindfulness has been found to be effective in reducing symptoms of ADHD and improving overall academic performance in children and students.

Finally, mindfulness has also been found to have a positive impact on relationships and social connections. By cultivating empathy and compassion, mindfulness can help to improve communication, reduce conflict, and build stronger, more meaningful connections with others.

In conclusion, the science of mindfulness is a rapidly growing field that has already produced a wealth of evidence supporting the many benefits of this ancient practice. Whether you're looking to improve your mental or physical health, manage stress and anxiety, improve your cognitive performance, or build stronger relationships, mindfulness is a powerful tool that can help you achieve your goals.

03: Understanding the Benefits of Mindfulness

Mindfulness is a powerful tool for personal growth and well-being that has been practiced for thousands of years. In recent years, scientific research has provided strong evidence supporting the many benefits of mindfulness, and today, millions of people around the world are using mindfulness to improve their mental and physical health, manage stress and anxiety, and achieve greater fulfillment in their personal and professional lives.

One of the key benefits of mindfulness is its ability to reduce stress and anxiety. In today's fast-paced, high-pressure world, many people struggle with feelings of overwhelm, anxiety, and stress. However, by practicing mindfulness, we can train our brains to be more resilient to these negative feelings and cultivate a state of inner peace and calm. This can have a profound impact on our mental and physical health, and can help us to feel more centered and balanced, even in the face of life's challenges.

Another important aspect of mindfulness is its impact on our relationships. By cultivating a greater sense of empathy and understanding, we can build stronger and more meaningful connections with the people in our lives. Mindfulness also helps us to communicate more effectively and to listen more deeply to others, which can lead to deeper, more authentic connections.

Mindfulness is also highly beneficial for our physical health. Research has shown that mindfulness can lower blood pressure, improve immune function, and reduce pain and inflammation. Additionally, mindfulness has been found to be an effective tool for managing chronic health conditions such as heart disease, cancer, and chronic pain.

In addition to its physical health benefits, mindfulness can also have a positive impact on our cognitive function. Studies have shown that mindfulness can improve attention, working memory, and executive function, making it an effective tool for improving overall cognitive performance. Additionally, mindfulness has been found to be effective in reducing symptoms of ADHD and improving overall academic performance in children and students.

Finally, mindfulness can also have a positive impact on our careers and our overall sense of purpose and fulfillment. By helping us to stay focused and centered, mindfulness can increase our productivity and creativity, and help us to be more effective in our work and more fulfilled in our personal lives.

In conclusion, mindfulness is a powerful tool for personal growth and well-being that offers a wide range of benefits for our mental, physical, and emotional health, as well as our relationships and careers. Whether you're looking to reduce stress and anxiety, build stronger relationships, or achieve greater fulfillment in your personal and professional life, mindfulness can help you to unlock the power of presence and achieve inner peace.

04: Mindfulness and Stress Management

Stress is a common and often unavoidable part of modern life, but left unchecked, it can lead to a host of negative consequences for our mental and physical health. However, by practicing mindfulness, we can develop the skills we need to manage stress and maintain a sense of calm and balance, even in the face of life's challenges.

One of the key ways that mindfulness helps to reduce stress is by training our brains to be more resilient to negative emotions and stressors. Through mindfulness practice, we learn to become more aware of our thoughts and feelings, and to approach them with a non-judgmental, accepting attitude. This can help us to develop greater emotional intelligence, and to better manage our reactions to stress and anxiety.

Additionally, mindfulness can help us to gain a better perspective on our stressors, and to develop more effective coping strategies. By becoming more aware of the thoughts and behaviors that trigger stress, we can learn to identify and change these patterns, and to develop healthier, more effective ways of managing stress.

04: MINDFULNESS AND STRESS MANAGEMENT

Another important aspect of mindfulness is its impact on physical health. Research has shown that mindfulness can lower blood pressure, improve immune function, and reduce pain and inflammation. Additionally, mindfulness has been found to be an effective tool for managing chronic health conditions such as heart disease, cancer, and chronic pain, which can further help to reduce stress and anxiety.

In addition to its physical health benefits, mindfulness can also have a positive impact on our mental health. By training the brain to be more resilient to stress and negative emotions, mindfulness can help to reduce symptoms of anxiety and depression, and improve overall emotional well-being. Additionally, mindfulness has been found to be an effective tool for managing symptoms of post-traumatic stress disorder (PTSD) and other mental health conditions.

Finally, mindfulness can also help us to maintain a better work-life balance, and to manage stress in the workplace. By helping us to stay focused and centered, mindfulness can increase our productivity and creativity, and help us to be more effective in our work and more fulfilled in our personal lives.

04: MINDFULNESS AND STRESS MANAGEMENT

In conclusion, mindfulness is a powerful tool for managing stress and anxiety, and for improving our overall mental and physical health. By cultivating a greater sense of presence, awareness, and compassion, mindfulness can help us to manage stress and maintain a sense of calm and balance, even in the face of life's challenges.

05: Mindfulness and Mental Health

Mental health is a critical aspect of our overall well-being, and it is important to take care of our mental health just as we take care of our physical health. Mindfulness is a powerful tool for improving mental health, and can help us to reduce symptoms of anxiety, depression, and other mental health conditions.

One of the key ways that mindfulness improves mental health is by reducing stress and anxiety. In today's fast-paced, high-pressure world, many people struggle with feelings of overwhelm, anxiety, and stress. However, by practicing mindfulness, we can train our brains to be more resilient to these negative feelings and cultivate a state of inner peace and calm. This can have a profound impact on our mental health and well-being, and can help us to feel more centered and balanced, even in the face of life's challenges.

Another important aspect of mindfulness is its impact on our emotional regulation. Through mindfulness practice, we can become more aware of our thoughts and feelings, and learn to approach them with a non-judgmental, accepting attitude. This can help us to better manage our emotions and to reduce symptoms of anxiety and depression.

Mindfulness has also been found to be an effective tool for managing symptoms of post-traumatic stress disorder (PTSD) and other mental health conditions. By helping us to better regulate our emotions and to gain greater insight into our thoughts and feelings, mindfulness can help us to overcome the negative thoughts and behaviors that contribute to mental health conditions.

Finally, mindfulness can also help us to maintain a better work-life balance, and to manage stress in the workplace. By helping us to stay focused and centered, mindfulness can increase our productivity and creativity, and help us to be more effective in our work and more fulfilled in our personal lives.

In conclusion, mindfulness is a powerful tool for improving mental health, and can help us to reduce symptoms of anxiety, depression, and other mental health conditions. By cultivating a greater sense of presence, awareness, and compassion, mindfulness can help us to better manage our emotions, regulate our thoughts and feelings, and achieve greater overall mental well-being.

06: Mindfulness and Physical Health

Physical health is an important aspect of our overall well-being, and it is essential that we take care of our bodies to maintain optimal health and vitality. Mindfulness is a powerful tool for improving physical health, and has been shown to have a number of positive effects on the body and mind.

One of the key ways that mindfulness improves physical health is by reducing stress and anxiety. Chronic stress and anxiety can have negative effects on the body, including increased blood pressure, weakened immune function, and increased inflammation. However, by practicing mindfulness, we can train our brains to be more resilient to these negative feelings and cultivate a state of inner peace and calm. This can help to reduce stress and improve physical health.

Mindfulness has also been found to be effective in managing chronic health conditions such as heart disease, cancer, and chronic pain. Through mindfulness practice, individuals with chronic health conditions can develop a greater sense of control over their symptoms, reduce stress and anxiety, and manage their conditions more effectively. Additionally, mindfulness has been shown to reduce pain and inflammation, improve immune function, and lower blood pressure, further contributing to improved physical health.

Another important aspect of mindfulness is its impact on sleep. Poor sleep is a common issue for many people, and can have negative consequences for physical health and well-being. However, mindfulness can help to improve sleep quality by reducing stress and anxiety and promoting relaxation. Additionally, mindfulness has been found to be effective in reducing symptoms of insomnia and sleep disorders.

Finally, mindfulness can also help us to maintain a healthy lifestyle, and to develop healthier habits and behaviors. By helping us to be more mindful of our thoughts and behaviors, mindfulness can help us to make better choices when it comes to our health and well-being, and to develop habits that promote physical health and vitality.

In conclusion, mindfulness is a powerful tool for improving physical health, and can help to reduce stress, manage chronic health conditions, improve sleep quality, and promote healthier habits and behaviors. By cultivating a greater sense of presence, awareness, and compassion, mindfulness can help us to achieve greater overall physical well-being and health.

07: Mindfulness and Emotional Intelligence

Emotional intelligence (EI) refers to the ability to understand and manage our own emotions and the emotions of others. It is a critical aspect of personal and professional success, and is essential for building strong relationships, managing conflict, and achieving personal and professional goals. Mindfulness is a powerful tool for improving emotional intelligence, and can help us to develop a greater understanding of our emotions and the emotions of others.

One of the key benefits of mindfulness is its impact on self-awareness. Through mindfulness practice, we can become more aware of our thoughts and feelings, and learn to approach them with a non-judgmental, accepting attitude. This can help us to better understand and manage our own emotions, and to increase our self-awareness and emotional intelligence.

Mindfulness also helps us to develop empathy and compassion for others, and to understand and manage the emotions of others. By practicing mindfulness, we can learn to put ourselves in the shoes of others, to understand their perspectives and feelings, and to respond to their emotions in a compassionate and understanding way. This can help us to build stronger relationships, to manage conflict more effectively, and to be more empathetic and compassionate towards others.

Additionally, mindfulness can help us to regulate our emotions, and to manage our emotions more effectively. By learning to manage our thoughts and feelings in a non-judgmental way, we can reduce stress and anxiety, and develop greater emotional stability. This can help us to respond to challenges and difficult situations more effectively, and to be more resilient in the face of emotional stress.

Finally, mindfulness can also help us to improve our communication skills, and to communicate more effectively with others. By helping us to understand our own emotions and the emotions of others, mindfulness can help us to communicate more effectively, to build stronger relationships, and to be more successful in our personal and professional lives.

In conclusion, mindfulness is a powerful tool for improving emotional intelligence, and can help us to develop greater self-awareness, empathy, and compassion, regulate our emotions, and improve our communication skills. By cultivating a greater sense of presence, awareness, and compassion, mindfulness can help us to achieve greater emotional intelligence and to be more successful in our personal and professional lives.

08: Mindfulness and Relationships

Relationships play a critical role in our lives, and are essential for our happiness, well-being, and sense of fulfillment. Mindfulness is a powerful tool for improving relationships, and can help us to build stronger, more fulfilling connections with others.

One of the key benefits of mindfulness is its impact on communication. Through mindfulness practice, we can become more aware of our thoughts and feelings, and learn to communicate them more effectively. This can help us to build stronger relationships by reducing misunderstandings and improving our ability to connect with others. Additionally, mindfulness can help us to develop better listening skills, to be more empathetic and compassionate towards others, and to respond to the needs and feelings of others in a more understanding and supportive way.

Mindfulness can also help us to manage conflict more effectively, and to resolve conflicts in a more positive and constructive way. By learning to regulate our emotions and approach conflicts with a non-judgmental attitude, we can reduce stress and anxiety, and find more effective and mutually beneficial solutions to conflicts.

Furthermore, mindfulness can help us to improve our relationships with others by promoting greater understanding and compassion. Through mindfulness practice, we can develop a greater appreciation for the perspectives and experiences of others, and learn to approach relationships with greater empathy and understanding. This can help us to build stronger, more meaningful connections with others, and to be more supportive and loving towards those we care about.

Finally, mindfulness can also help us to improve our relationships with ourselves, and to cultivate a greater sense of self-love and self-acceptance. By learning to be more mindful of our thoughts and feelings, we can develop a greater sense of self-awareness and self-compassion, and learn to be more accepting and loving towards ourselves. This can help us to be more confident and secure in our relationships with others, and to cultivate a more fulfilling and satisfying life.

In conclusion, mindfulness is a powerful tool for improving relationships, and can help us to build stronger, more fulfilling connections with others, manage conflict more effectively, promote greater understanding and compassion, and improve our relationships with ourselves. By cultivating a greater sense of presence, awareness, and compassion, mindfulness can help us to achieve greater satisfaction and fulfillment in our relationships and in our lives.

09: Mindfulness and Workplace Success

The modern workplace can be fast-paced and stressful, and it's essential to have effective tools and strategies to manage stress, increase productivity, and achieve success. Mindfulness is a powerful tool that can help individuals achieve greater success in the workplace, by improving focus, reducing stress, and promoting well-being.

One of the key benefits of mindfulness is its impact on focus and attention. By practicing mindfulness, individuals can learn to focus their attention more effectively, and to avoid distractions and interruptions that can interfere with productivity. This can help individuals to be more productive, to complete tasks more efficiently, and to achieve their goals in a more timely manner.

Mindfulness also helps individuals to manage stress more effectively, by reducing feelings of anxiety, worry, and burnout. By learning to approach stress in a non-judgmental way, individuals can reduce the negative impact of stress on their well-being, and increase their ability to respond to challenges and difficult situations in a more positive and effective way.

09: MINDFULNESS AND WORKPLACE SUCCESS

In addition, mindfulness can help individuals to develop better communication skills, and to interact with others more effectively. By becoming more aware of their own thoughts and feelings, individuals can communicate more clearly and effectively, and build stronger relationships with colleagues, clients, and customers. This can help individuals to achieve greater success in the workplace, and to be more successful in their professional lives.

Finally, mindfulness can also help individuals to cultivate a greater sense of well-being and happiness, which can have a positive impact on their work performance and success. By learning to approach life with a non-judgmental and accepting attitude, individuals can reduce feelings of stress and anxiety, and increase their overall happiness and satisfaction.

In conclusion, mindfulness is a powerful tool for workplace success, and can help individuals to increase focus, reduce stress, improve communication, and cultivate a greater sense of well-being and happiness. By incorporating mindfulness into their daily routines, individuals can achieve greater success in the workplace, and lead more fulfilling and satisfying lives.

10: Mindfulness and Creativity

Creativity is an essential aspect of human life, and is essential for personal growth, innovation, and progress. Mindfulness is a powerful tool for unlocking creativity and fostering greater creativity in our lives.

One of the key benefits of mindfulness is its impact on our ability to think and problem-solve. By practicing mindfulness, we can become more aware of our thoughts and emotions, and learn to approach challenges and problems in a more open and flexible way. This can help us to find new and innovative solutions to problems, and to tap into our creativity in new and exciting ways.

Mindfulness also helps to reduce stress and anxiety, which can have a negative impact on our ability to be creative. By reducing feelings of stress and anxiety, we can increase our ability to think and problem-solve in a more effective and innovative way, and to pursue creative projects and endeavors with greater enthusiasm and success.

Additionally, mindfulness can help us to develop a greater sense of self-awareness and self-reflection, which can be critical for unlocking our creative potential. By becoming more aware of our thoughts, feelings, and experiences, we can gain a deeper understanding of ourselves and our creat-ive potential, and learn to channel our creative energies in new and exciting ways.

Finally, mindfulness can also help us to be more open and receptive to new ideas and experiences, which can be essen-tial for fostering creativity. By approaching life with an open and non-judgmental attitude, we can become more recept-ive to new ideas and experiences, and to new ways of think-ing and problem-solving.

In conclusion, mindfulness is a powerful tool for fostering creativity, and can help us to think more openly and creat-ively, reduce stress and anxiety, develop a greater sense of self-awareness and self-reflection, and be more open and receptive to new ideas and experiences. By incorporating mindfulness into our daily lives, we can unlock our creative potential, and lead more fulfilling and exciting lives.

11: Mindfulness and Focus

Focus is an essential aspect of human life, and is critical for achieving success in our personal and professional lives. Mindfulness is a powerful tool for improving focus and concentration, and for helping individuals to achieve their goals more effectively.

One of the key benefits of mindfulness is its impact on our ability to focus and concentrate. By practicing mindfulness, we can learn to focus our attention more effectively, and to avoid distractions and interruptions that can interfere with productivity. This can help us to be more productive, to complete tasks more efficiently, and to achieve our goals in a more timely manner.

In addition, mindfulness can help us to reduce feelings of stress and anxiety, which can have a negative impact on our focus and concentration. By reducing stress and anxiety, we can increase our ability to focus and concentrate, and to perform at our best in all areas of life.

Furthermore, mindfulness can help us to develop a greater sense of self-awareness, and to understand the patterns of thinking and behavior that can interfere with our ability to focus and concentrate. By becoming more aware of our thoughts, feelings, and experiences, we can learn to interrupt these patterns, and to focus our attention more effectively.

Finally, mindfulness can also help us to cultivate a sense of calm and clarity, which can be essential for improving focus and concentration. By developing a sense of inner peace and tranquility, we can increase our ability to focus and concentrate, and to perform at our best in all areas of life.

In conclusion, mindfulness is a powerful tool for improving focus and concentration, and can help us to be more productive, reduce stress and anxiety, develop a greater sense of self-awareness, and cultivate a sense of calm and clarity. By incorporating mindfulness into our daily lives, we can achieve our goals more effectively, and lead more fulfilling and successful lives.

12: Mindfulness and Decision Making

Making effective decisions is a critical aspect of human life, and can have a profound impact on our happiness, well-being, and success. Mindfulness is a powerful tool for improving decision making, and for helping individuals to make better, more informed choices.

One of the key benefits of mindfulness is its impact on our ability to think and process information more effectively. By practicing mindfulness, we can become more aware of our thoughts, emotions, and biases, and learn to approach problems and decisions in a more objective and rational way. This can help us to make more informed and effective decisions, and to avoid making impulsive or emotionally driven choices.

In addition, mindfulness can help us to reduce stress and anxiety, which can have a negative impact on our ability to make decisions effectively. By reducing stress and anxiety, we can increase our ability to think and process information more effectively, and to make decisions that are in line with our values and goals.

Furthermore, mindfulness can help us to develop a greater sense of self-awareness and self-reflection, which can be critical for making effective decisions. By becoming more aware of our thoughts, feelings, and experiences, we can gain a deeper understanding of ourselves, and learn to make decisions that are in line with our values, goals, and priorities.

Finally, mindfulness can also help us to cultivate a sense of calm and clarity, which can be essential for making effective decisions. By developing a sense of inner peace and tranquility, we can increase our ability to think and process information more effectively, and to make decisions that are in line with our values, goals, and priorities.

In conclusion, mindfulness is a powerful tool for improving decision making, and can help us to think and process information more effectively, reduce stress and anxiety, develop a greater sense of self-awareness and self-reflection, and cultivate a sense of calm and clarity. By incorporating mindfulness into our daily lives, we can make better, more informed decisions, and lead more fulfilling and successful lives.

13: Mindfulness and Self-Acceptance

Self-acceptance is a critical aspect of human well-being and happiness, and is essential for leading a fulfilling and meaningful life. Mindfulness is a powerful tool for improving self-acceptance, and for helping individuals to develop a deeper sense of self-awareness, self-compassion, and self-love.

One of the key benefits of mindfulness is its impact on our ability to become more aware of our thoughts, emotions, and experiences. By practicing mindfulness, we can learn to observe our thoughts and emotions in a non-judgmental way, and to gain a deeper understanding of ourselves and our experiences. This can help us to develop a greater sense of self-awareness, and to accept ourselves for who we are, warts and all.

In addition, mindfulness can help us to reduce feelings of stress and anxiety, which can have a negative impact on our self-esteem and self-worth. By reducing stress and anxiety, we can increase our ability to feel good about ourselves, and to develop a greater sense of self-confidence and self-acceptance.

Furthermore, mindfulness can help us to cultivate a sense of self-compassion and self-love, which are critical for improving self-acceptance. By becoming more aware of our thoughts, feelings, and experiences, and by treating ourselves with kindness, compassion, and understanding, we can learn to accept ourselves for who we are, and to develop a deeper sense of self-love and self-acceptance.

Finally, mindfulness can also help us to develop a greater sense of gratitude and appreciation, which can be essential for improving self-acceptance. By cultivating a sense of gratitude and appreciation, we can learn to focus on our strengths, gifts, and talents, and to appreciate and accept ourselves for who we are.

In conclusion, mindfulness is a powerful tool for improving self-acceptance, and can help us to become more aware of our thoughts, emotions, and experiences, reduce stress and anxiety, cultivate self-compassion and self-love, and develop a sense of gratitude and appreciation. By incorporating mindfulness into our daily lives, we can develop a deeper sense of self-awareness, self-compassion, and self-acceptance, and lead more fulfilling and meaningful lives.

14: Mindfulness and Gratitude

Gratitude is a powerful emotion that has the ability to improve our well-being, increase our happiness, and enhance our relationships with others. Mindfulness is a complementary practice that can amplify the benefits of gratitude, by helping us to cultivate a greater sense of awareness, presence, and compassion in our daily lives.

Studies have shown that cultivating gratitude can have a positive impact on our physical and mental health, by reducing symptoms of stress, anxiety, and depression, and improving our sleep and overall mood. Mindfulness can enhance these benefits, by helping us to focus our attention on the present moment and to appreciate the small things in life that often go unnoticed.

Mindfulness and gratitude are interlinked, as practicing mindfulness can help us to become more aware of the things that we are grateful for, and to feel gratitude more deeply. By paying attention to our thoughts, emotions, and experiences in a non-judgmental way, we can develop a greater sense of gratitude for what we have, and for the people in our lives.

In addition, mindfulness can also help us to overcome negative thought patterns that may be blocking our ability to experience gratitude. For example, if we are feeling overwhelmed with stress or anxiety, we may find it difficult to focus on the things that we are grateful for. However, by practicing mindfulness, we can learn to become more aware of these negative thoughts and emotions, and to let them go, allowing us to cultivate a sense of gratitude and joy.

Moreover, practicing mindfulness can also help us to develop a greater sense of empathy and compassion, which are critical components of gratitude. By becoming more aware of the experiences of others, and by treating others with kindness and compassion, we can develop stronger relationships and deeper connections with those around us, and experience a greater sense of gratitude for the people in our lives.

Finally, mindfulness can help us to develop a sense of gratitude for the present moment, and to appreciate the simple things in life. By focusing on the present moment and by appreciating the things that we have, we can live in the moment and experience a greater sense of joy, happiness, and well-being.

14: MINDFULNESS AND GRATITUDE

In conclusion, mindfulness and gratitude are powerful practices that can enhance our well-being, increase our happiness, and improve our relationships with others. By incorporating mindfulness and gratitude into our daily lives, we can develop a deeper sense of awareness, presence, and compassion, and live more fulfilling and meaningful lives.

15: Mindfulness and Forgiveness

Forgiveness is an essential aspect of personal growth and well-being, and mindfulness can play a key role in facilitating this process. Forgiveness involves letting go of grudges, resentment, and negative emotions that can hold us back, and embracing a more positive and compassionate outlook on life.

Mindfulness can help us to become more aware of the negative emotions and thought patterns that may be preventing us from forgiving others and ourselves. By paying attention to our thoughts and emotions in a non-judgmental way, we can gain a deeper understanding of why we are feeling angry, resentful, or hurt, and take steps to overcome these negative emotions.

Furthermore, mindfulness can also help us to cultivate a greater sense of compassion, empathy, and understanding, which are critical components of forgiveness. By becoming more aware of the experiences of others, and by treating others with kindness and compassion, we can develop a deeper understanding of why they may have acted in a certain way, and find it easier to forgive them.

In addition, mindfulness can also help us to let go of negative thoughts and emotions, and to focus on the present moment. By letting go of the past and focusing on the present, we can free ourselves from the negative emotions that may be preventing us from forgiving others, and find it easier to move forward in a positive and productive way.

Moreover, practicing mindfulness can also help us to develop a greater sense of self-awareness, self-acceptance, and self-compassion, which are essential components of forgiving ourselves. By becoming more aware of our own thoughts and emotions, and by treating ourselves with kindness and compassion, we can develop a greater understanding of our own motivations, behaviors, and experiences, and find it easier to forgive ourselves for our mistakes.

Finally, mindfulness can help us to cultivate a sense of gratitude, which can also play a role in fostering forgiveness. By focusing on the things that we are grateful for, and by appreciating the good in our lives, we can develop a more positive and compassionate outlook, and find it easier to forgive others and ourselves.

In conclusion, mindfulness and forgiveness are powerful practices that can enhance our well-being, increase our happiness, and improve our relationships with others. By incorporating mindfulness and forgiveness into our daily lives, we can develop a deeper sense of awareness, presence, and compassion, and live more fulfilling and meaningful lives.

16: Mindfulness and Compassion

Compassion is a key aspect of personal growth and well-being, and mindfulness can play a crucial role in fostering this essential quality. Compassion involves recognizing and responding to the suffering of others with kindness, understanding, and a desire to help.

Mindfulness can help us to cultivate a deeper understanding of the experiences of others, and to develop a greater capacity for empathy and compassion. By paying attention to our thoughts and emotions in a non-judgmental way, we can gain a deeper understanding of our own experiences, and develop a greater appreciation for the experiences of others.

Furthermore, mindfulness can help us to cultivate a greater sense of self-awareness, which is an essential component of compassion. By becoming more aware of our own thoughts and emotions, we can better understand our own motivations, behaviors, and experiences, and develop a greater capacity for empathy and compassion towards others.

Moreover, mindfulness can also help us to overcome negative emotions and thought patterns that may be preventing us from being compassionate. For example, by paying attention to our thoughts and emotions in a non-judgmental way, we can become more aware of our own prejudices, biases, and negative emotions, and take steps to overcome these obstacles to compassion.

In addition, practicing mindfulness can also help us to cultivate a greater sense of gratitude, which can also play a role in fostering compassion. By focusing on the things that we are grateful for, and by appreciating the good in our lives, we can develop a more positive and compassionate outlook, and find it easier to extend compassion towards others.

Finally, mindfulness can help us to overcome the barriers to compassion, such as fear, anger, and resentment. By becoming more aware of these emotions and learning to overcome them, we can develop a deeper sense of compassion, and live more fulfilling and meaningful lives.

In conclusion, mindfulness and compassion are powerful practices that can enhance our well-being, increase our happiness, and improve our relationships with others. By incorporating mindfulness and compassion into our daily lives, we can develop a deeper sense of awareness, presence, and compassion, and live more fulfilling and meaningful lives.

17: Mindfulness and Positive Thinking

Positive thinking is a powerful tool for enhancing well-being and achieving success in life. By focusing on positive thoughts, feelings, and experiences, we can create a more positive and optimistic outlook, and reduce stress, anxiety, and depression.

Mindfulness is an effective tool for promoting positive thinking, as it can help us to become more aware of our thoughts and emotions, and to cultivate a more positive outlook. By paying attention to our thoughts and emotions in a non-judgmental way, we can become more aware of negative thoughts and emotions, and take steps to overcome them.

Moreover, mindfulness can help us to cultivate gratitude and appreciation, which are essential components of positive thinking. By paying attention to the good things in our lives, and by focusing on what we are grateful for, we can develop a more positive and optimistic outlook, and reduce stress, anxiety, and depression.

In addition, mindfulness can also help us to overcome negative thought patterns and limiting beliefs, such as perfectionism, low self-esteem, and self-doubt. By becoming more aware of these thoughts and beliefs, we can take steps to overcome them, and develop a more positive and optimistic outlook.

Furthermore, mindfulness can help us to cultivate a sense of purpose and meaning in life, which is an essential component of positive thinking. By becoming more aware of our values, goals, and aspirations, we can find greater fulfillment and satisfaction in life, and develop a more positive and optimistic outlook.

Finally, mindfulness can also help us to cultivate resilience, which is an essential component of positive thinking. By becoming more aware of our thoughts and emotions, and by learning to regulate our emotions, we can develop greater resilience, and find it easier to overcome life's challenges and setbacks.

In conclusion, mindfulness and positive thinking are powerful tools for enhancing well-being and achieving success in life. By incorporating mindfulness and positive thinking into our daily lives, we can cultivate a more positive and optimistic outlook, and live more fulfilling and meaningful lives.

18: Mindfulness and Mindful Communication

Mindful communication is the art of communicating in a way that is intentional, authentic, and respectful. It involves paying attention to our thoughts, feelings, and emotions, and to the thoughts, feelings, and emotions of others. By becoming more mindful in our communication, we can improve our relationships, reduce stress and conflict, and create a more positive and supportive environment.

Mindfulness is an essential tool for promoting mindful communication, as it can help us to become more aware of our thoughts and emotions, and to communicate in a more intentional, authentic, and respectful way. By paying attention to our thoughts and emotions in a non-judgmental way, we can become more aware of our communication patterns, and take steps to improve them.

Moreover, mindfulness can help us to develop greater empathy and compassion, which are essential components of mindful communication. By becoming more aware of the thoughts, feelings, and emotions of others, we can develop a deeper understanding of their perspectives, and communicate in a more understanding and compassionate way.

In addition, mindfulness can help us to cultivate active listening, which is an essential component of mindful communication. By paying attention to what others are saying, and by responding in a thoughtful and respectful way, we can create a more positive and supportive environment, and reduce stress and conflict.

Furthermore, mindfulness can help us to overcome communication barriers, such as defensiveness, anger, and frustration. By becoming more aware of our thoughts and emotions, and by learning to regulate our emotions, we can communicate more effectively, and reduce stress and conflict.

Finally, mindfulness can also help us to cultivate assertiveness, which is an essential component of mindful communication. By becoming more aware of our thoughts, feelings, and emotions, and by learning to express them in a clear and confident way, we can communicate more effectively, and reduce stress and conflict.

In conclusion, mindfulness and mindful communication are powerful tools for enhancing our relationships, reducing stress and conflict, and creating a more positive and supportive environment. By incorporating mindfulness and mindful communication into our daily lives, we can improve our relationships, and live more fulfilling and meaningful lives.

19: Mindfulness and Mindful Listening

Mindful listening is the act of paying attention to the words and emotions of others in a non-judgmental and compassionate way. It is a crucial component of mindful communication, and can help us to improve our relationships, reduce stress and conflict, and create a more positive and supportive environment.

Mindfulness is an essential tool for promoting mindful listening, as it helps us to become more aware of our thoughts, feelings, and emotions, and to listen more intentionally, authentically, and respectfully. By paying attention to our thoughts and emotions in a non-judgmental way, we can become more aware of our listening patterns, and take steps to improve them.

Moreover, mindfulness can help us to cultivate empathy and compassion, which are essential components of mindful listening. By becoming more aware of the thoughts, feelings, and emotions of others, we can develop a deeper understanding of their perspectives, and listen in a more understanding and compassionate way.

19: MINDFULNESS AND MINDFUL LISTENING

In addition, mindfulness can help us to overcome listening barriers, such as distraction, judgment, and defensiveness. By becoming more aware of our thoughts and emotions, and by learning to regulate our emotions, we can listen more effectively, and reduce stress and conflict.

Furthermore, mindfulness can also help us to cultivate active listening, which is an essential component of mindful listening. By paying attention to what others are saying, and by responding in a thoughtful and respectful way, we can create a more positive and supportive environment, and reduce stress and conflict.

Finally, mindfulness can also help us to develop deeper relationships, as it allows us to listen in a more intentional, authentic, and respectful way. By paying attention to what others are saying, and by responding in a thoughtful and respectful way, we can create deeper and more meaningful connections, and improve our relationships.

In conclusion, mindfulness and mindful listening are powerful tools for enhancing our relationships, reducing stress and conflict, and creating a more positive and supportive environment. By incorporating mindfulness and mindful listening into our daily lives, we can improve our relationships, and live more fulfilling and meaningful lives.

20: Mindfulness and Mindful Eating

Mindful eating is the act of paying attention to the experience of eating, including the food itself, our thoughts, emotions, and physical sensations. This approach to eating can help us to reduce stress and anxiety, promote healthy eating habits, and improve our overall physical and mental health.

Mindfulness is a key component of mindful eating, as it helps us to become more aware of our thoughts, emotions, and physical sensations. By paying attention to these experiences, we can learn to tune into our hunger and fullness cues, and make more informed decisions about what, when, and how much to eat.

Moreover, mindfulness can help us to reduce stress and anxiety associated with eating, as it helps us to focus on the present moment, rather than dwelling on the past or worrying about the future. By paying attention to our thoughts and emotions, and by practicing self-compassion, we can reduce stress and anxiety, and promote a more positive and healthy relationship with food.

In addition, mindfulness can also help us to overcome disordered eating patterns, such as overeating, binge eating, and emotional eating. By becoming more aware of our thoughts and emotions, and by learning to regulate our emotions, we can reduce the likelihood of engaging in disordered eating behaviors.

Furthermore, mindfulness can also help us to develop healthier eating habits, such as reducing mindless snacking, reducing distractions while eating, and focusing on nutrient-dense foods. By paying attention to our physical sensations and eating experiences, we can make more informed decisions about what, when, and how much to eat.

Finally, mindfulness can also help us to cultivate gratitude and appreciation for the food we eat, and to develop a more mindful and intentional relationship with food. By paying attention to the flavors, textures, and aromas of food, we can appreciate the food we eat more deeply, and develop a more positive and healthy relationship with food.

In conclusion, mindfulness and mindful eating are powerful tools for promoting healthy eating habits, reducing stress and anxiety associated with eating, and improving our overall physical and mental health. By incorporating mindfulness and mindful eating into our daily lives, we can develop a more positive and healthy relationship with food, and improve our overall well-being.

21: Mindfulness and Mindful Breathing

Mindful breathing is a simple yet powerful practice that involves paying attention to the sensation of breathing. This practice can help us to reduce stress and anxiety, improve our physical and mental health, and cultivate a sense of inner peace and calm.

Mindfulness is an important component of mindful breathing, as it helps us to become more aware of our thoughts, emotions, and physical sensations. By focusing on the sensation of breathing, we can bring our attention to the present moment, and reduce stress and anxiety by calming the mind and body.

Mindful breathing can also help us to improve our physical health, as it can help to lower blood pressure, reduce heart rate, and improve respiratory function. This practice can also help us to manage physical symptoms associated with stress and anxiety, such as headaches, muscle tension, and digestive problems.

In addition, mindful breathing can also help us to develop a greater sense of inner peace and calm, by calming the mind and reducing stress and anxiety. By taking a few minutes each day to focus on our breathing, we can cultivate a sense of inner peace, and develop a more positive and healthy relationship with stress and anxiety.

Furthermore, mindful breathing can also help us to cultivate greater self-awareness, by helping us to become more aware of our thoughts, emotions, and physical sensations. This can help us to make more informed decisions about how we respond to stress and anxiety, and to develop more effective coping strategies for managing stress and anxiety.

Finally, mindful breathing can also help us to cultivate greater compassion and kindness towards ourselves and others. By paying attention to the sensations of breathing, and by practicing self-compassion, we can develop a more positive and healthy relationship with ourselves and others, and cultivate greater compassion and kindness towards others.

In conclusion, mindful breathing is a simple and effective practice for reducing stress and anxiety, improving physical and mental health, and cultivating inner peace and calm. By incorporating mindful breathing into our daily lives, we can develop a more positive and healthy relationship with stress and anxiety, and improve our overall well-being.

22: Mindfulness and Body Awareness

Body awareness is an important aspect of mindfulness practice, as it involves paying attention to the sensations and feelings in our bodies. This practice can help us to become more in tune with our physical selves, and to develop a deeper understanding of the connection between our bodies and our minds.

Mindfulness and body awareness are closely related, as mindfulness involves paying attention to the present moment, including our thoughts, emotions, and physical sensations. By becoming more aware of the sensations in our bodies, we can develop a deeper understanding of our physical and emotional responses to stress and anxiety, and learn to manage these responses more effectively.

One of the key benefits of body awareness is that it can help us to reduce stress and anxiety. By paying attention to the sensations in our bodies, we can become more aware of the physical symptoms of stress and anxiety, such as muscle tension, headaches, and digestive problems. By recognizing these symptoms, we can learn to manage them more effectively, and reduce the impact of stress and anxiety on our lives.

In addition, body awareness can also help us to improve our physical health. By paying attention to the sensations in our bodies, we can become more aware of physical symptoms that may indicate a health issue, such as pain, discomfort, or changes in our energy levels. By becoming more aware of these symptoms, we can seek medical attention if necessary, and take steps to improve our physical health.

Body awareness can also help us to develop greater self-awareness, by helping us to become more in tune with our physical selves. This can help us to make more informed decisions about our physical and emotional well-being, and to develop more effective coping strategies for managing stress and anxiety.

Furthermore, body awareness can also help us to develop greater compassion and kindness towards ourselves and others. By paying attention to the sensations in our bodies, and by practicing self-compassion, we can develop a more positive and healthy relationship with ourselves and others, and cultivate greater compassion and kindness towards others.

22: MINDFULNESS AND BODY AWARENESS

In conclusion, body awareness is a valuable aspect of mindfulness practice, as it involves paying attention to the sensations and feelings in our bodies. By incorporating body awareness into our mindfulness practice, we can reduce stress and anxiety, improve our physical health, develop greater self-awareness, and cultivate greater compassion and kindness towards ourselves and others.

23: Mindfulness and Meditation

Meditation is an ancient practice that has been used for centuries to cultivate mindfulness, increase self-awareness, and promote physical, emotional, and mental well-being. Today, meditation is widely recognized as an effective tool for reducing stress and anxiety, improving mental clarity and focus, and enhancing overall well-being.

Mindfulness and meditation are closely related, as mindfulness is an essential aspect of meditation practice. In meditation, we use mindfulness to focus our attention on the present moment, and to develop a deeper understanding of our thoughts, emotions, and physical sensations. By practicing mindfulness in meditation, we can cultivate a sense of peace and calm, and develop greater self-awareness and self-compassion.

There are many different types of meditation, each with its own unique focus and approach. Some forms of meditation focus on mindfulness, while others focus on visualization, mantras, or other techniques. Some common forms of meditation include mindfulness meditation, loving-kindness meditation, and body scan meditation.

One of the key benefits of meditation is that it can help us to reduce stress and anxicty. By taking time to focus our attention on the present moment and to cultivate mindfulness, we can reduce the impact of stress and anxiety on our lives, and develop more effective coping strategies for managing these challenges.

In addition, meditation can also improve our mental clarity and focus. By developing a deeper awareness of our thoughts and emotions, we can become more centered and focused, and more effective in our personal and professional lives.

Meditation can also help us to develop greater self-awareness and self-compassion. By taking time to focus on our thoughts, emotions, and physical sensations, we can become more aware of our patterns of thinking and behavior, and develop a more positive and healthy relationship with ourselves.

Furthermore, meditation can also have a positive impact on our physical health. Studies have shown that regular meditation practice can lower blood pressure, reduce chronic pain, improve sleep quality, and enhance overall physical well-being.

23: MINDFULNESS AND MEDITATION

In conclusion, meditation is an effective tool for cultivating mindfulness, reducing stress and anxiety, improving mental clarity and focus, and enhancing overall well-being. By incorporating meditation into our mindfulness practice, we can cultivate a sense of peace and calm, and develop greater self-awareness and self-compassion.

24: Mindfulness and Yoga

Yoga is an ancient practice that has been used for thousands of years to promote physical, mental, and spiritual well-being. Yoga is a holistic practice that integrates the mind, body, and spirit, and it has become increasingly popular in recent years as a tool for promoting mindfulness and reducing stress.

Mindfulness and yoga are closely related, as mindfulness is an essential aspect of the yoga practice. In yoga, we use mindfulness to focus our attention on the present moment, and to cultivate a deeper understanding of our thoughts, emotions, and physical sensations. By practicing mindfulness in yoga, we can develop a deeper sense of self-awareness, and enhance our physical, mental, and emotional well-being.

Yoga incorporates a variety of physical postures, breathing exercises, and meditation techniques, each of which is designed to promote mindfulness and well-being. Some of the key benefits of yoga include reducing stress and anxiety, improving physical flexibility and strength, and enhancing overall physical and mental well-being.

One of the key benefits of yoga is its ability to reduce stress and anxiety. By focusing our attention on the present moment and cultivating mindfulness, we can reduce the impact of stress and anxiety on our lives, and develop more effective coping strategies for managing these challenges.

In addition, yoga can also improve our physical health. By practicing a variety of physical postures, we can increase our physical strength, flexibility, and balance, and improve our overall physical well-being. Regular yoga practice can also help to improve posture, reduce chronic pain, and increase energy levels.

Furthermore, yoga can also have a positive impact on our mental health. By cultivating mindfulness and developing a deeper self-awareness, we can enhance our emotional well-being, improve our mental clarity and focus, and increase our sense of peace and calm.

In conclusion, yoga is a powerful tool for promoting mindfulness and well-being. By incorporating yoga into our mindfulness practice, we can cultivate a deeper sense of self-awareness, reduce stress and anxiety, improve physical health, and enhance overall well-being. Whether we are seeking to improve our physical fitness, reduce stress and anxiety, or enhance our mental clarity and focus, yoga provides a holistic approach to well-being that can help us to achieve our goals and live a more fulfilling life.

25: Mindfulness and Nature

Nature has always had a profound impact on human well-being, and the connection between mindfulness and nature is becoming increasingly recognized. Practicing mindfulness in nature can help us to cultivate a deeper sense of presence, and to improve our overall physical, mental, and emotional health.

The benefits of nature and mindfulness are numerous, and include reducing stress and anxiety, improving mood and cognitive function, and enhancing our sense of peace and calm. By spending time in nature and practicing mindfulness, we can create a deeper connection with the world around us, and tap into the healing power of the natural world.

One of the key benefits of mindfulness in nature is its ability to reduce stress and anxiety. Research has shown that spending time in nature and practicing mindfulness can lower levels of the stress hormone cortisol, and help us to cope more effectively with life's challenges. Furthermore, by practicing mindfulness in nature, we can increase our sense of calm, reduce feelings of anger and frustration, and improve our overall well-being.

In addition, mindfulness in nature can also improve our physical health. Spending time in nature can increase our physical activity levels, improve our sleep, and reduce symptoms of chronic pain. By practicing mindfulness in nature, we can also improve our focus and attention, and enhance our cognitive function.

Furthermore, mindfulness in nature can also have a positive impact on our mental health. Research has shown that spending time in nature can improve our mood, reduce feelings of depression and anxiety, and increase our overall sense of well-being. By practicing mindfulness in nature, we can also cultivate a deeper sense of self-awareness, and enhance our emotional intelligence.

In conclusion, mindfulness in nature is a powerful tool for improving well-being. Whether we are seeking to reduce stress and anxiety, improve our physical health, or enhance our mental clarity and focus, practicing mindfulness in nature can help us to achieve our goals and live a more fulfilling life. Whether it is taking a walk in the park, sitting by a lake, or simply observing the beauty of nature, the combination of mindfulness and nature has the power to transform our lives, and to bring greater peace, happiness, and well-being into our lives.

26: Mindfulness and Music

Music is a powerful tool for personal growth and well-being, and when combined with mindfulness, it can bring about significant positive changes in our lives. Music has the ability to evoke emotions, to reduce stress and anxiety, and to bring us into a deeper state of relaxation and calm. By incorporating mindfulness into our relationship with music, we can enhance its therapeutic benefits and use it as a tool for personal transformation.

The benefits of mindfulness and music are numerous, and include reducing stress and anxiety, improving sleep, and enhancing our sense of well-being. Research has shown that listening to music can have a profound impact on our mental and emotional state, and that incorporating mindfulness into our listening practice can deepen its effects.

One of the key benefits of mindfulness and music is its ability to reduce stress and anxiety. Studies have shown that listening to music can lower levels of the stress hormone cortisol, and help us to cope more effectively with life's challenges. Furthermore, by practicing mindfulness while listening to music, we can increase our awareness of our thoughts and emotions, and learn to manage our stress in a more effective and healthy way.

In addition, mindfulness and music can also improve our physical health. Research has shown that listening to music can increase our physical activity levels, improve our sleep, and reduce symptoms of chronic pain. By practicing mindfulness while listening to music, we can also enhance our focus and attention, and improve our cognitive function.

Furthermore, mindfulness and music can also have a positive impact on our mental health. Studies have shown that listening to music can improve our mood, reduce feelings of depression and anxiety, and increase our overall sense of well-being. By practicing mindfulness while listening to music, we can also cultivate a deeper sense of self-awareness, and enhance our emotional intelligence.

In conclusion, mindfulness and music are a powerful combination for personal growth and well-being. Whether we are seeking to reduce stress and anxiety, improve our physical health, or enhance our mental clarity and focus, practicing mindfulness while listening to music can help us to achieve our goals and live a more fulfilling life. Whether it is listening to classical music, enjoying a playlist, or simply sitting in silence and listening to the sounds of nature, the combination of mindfulness and music has the power to transform our lives, and to bring greater peace, happiness, and well-being into our lives.

27: Mindfulness and Art

Art is a powerful tool for exploring our emotions and thoughts. It can help us to understand ourselves better, and to develop mindfulness skills. In this chapter, we will examine how mindfulness and art intersect, and how practicing mindfulness can help to enhance our creative abilities.

Mindfulness and art share several important elements. Both mindfulness and art involve a focus on the present moment, an openness to experience, and an awareness of our own thoughts and feelings. When we practice mindfulness, we cultivate a sense of curiosity and non-judgment, which can help us to tap into our innate creativity.

Art is a form of self-expression that can be used to explore our inner world. When we engage in artistic activities, such as drawing, painting, or sculpting, we are able to connect with our emotions and thoughts in a new way. This can help us to process and understand them better, and to develop a greater awareness of our own mental and emotional states.

In addition, mindfulness practices such as meditation and yoga can help to cultivate focus, which is a key component of creative expression. When we are able to quiet our minds and maintain a sense of presence, we are better able to access our intuition and to express our unique perspective.

Another way in which mindfulness and art intersect is in their shared focus on the present moment. Artistic activities require us to be fully engaged in the moment, which can help us to cultivate mindfulness skills. This can be especially beneficial for individuals who struggle with anxiety or depression, as it provides a distraction from negative thoughts and feelings, and can help to promote feelings of relaxation and calm.

Finally, practicing mindfulness can help to enhance our appreciation of art. When we are present and mindful, we are better able to fully experience the beauty and meaning of a piece of art. This can deepen our connection with the art, and with the artist, and can enrich our overall experience of life.

In conclusion, mindfulness and art are complementary practices that can help us to tap into our creativity and to cultivate a greater sense of self-awareness and inner peace. By incorporating mindfulness into our artistic pursuits, we can deepen our connection with the world around us, and with ourselves, and can enhance our overall well-being.

28: Mindfulness and Sleep

Sleep is a critical aspect of our physical and mental well-being, yet many of us struggle to get enough of it or suffer from sleep problems such as insomnia. Fortunately, mindfulness can be an effective tool in helping to improve sleep quality and quantity.

The first step in using mindfulness for better sleep is to become aware of our current sleep habits and patterns. This might involve keeping a sleep diary or tracking our sleep with a sleep monitoring device. Once we have a good understanding of our sleep patterns, we can then start to explore how mindfulness can help us to get better sleep.

One of the most effective ways to use mindfulness for sleep is through mindfulness-based stress reduction (MBSR) techniques. MBSR involves training our mind to focus on the present moment and to let go of thoughts and worries that can prevent us from getting a good night's sleep. This can be done through practices such as meditation, yoga, and deep breathing exercises.

Another way to use mindfulness for sleep is through mindful breathing exercises. These exercises involve focusing on the sensation of our breath as we inhale and exhale, helping us to calm our mind and reduce stress and anxiety that can interfere with sleep. These exercises can be done just before bedtime to help prepare our mind and body for sleep, or during the night if we wake up and find it difficult to get back to sleep.

Finally, practicing mindfulness in daily activities such as eating, walking, or even brushing our teeth can help us to cultivate a greater awareness of our bodies and our environment, which can translate into better sleep. When we are more in tune with our bodies and our surroundings, we are more likely to notice physical sensations and sounds that may disrupt our sleep and take steps to minimize them.

In conclusion, mindfulness can be a powerful tool in improving sleep quality and quantity. Whether through mindfulness-based stress reduction techniques, mindful breathing exercises, or cultivating mindfulness in our daily activities, incorporating mindfulness into our sleep routine can help us to get better, more restful sleep.

29: Mindfulness and Exercise

Exercise is a key component of a healthy lifestyle, but it can also be a powerful tool for cultivating mindfulness. When we engage in physical activity, we give our minds a break from the constant stream of thoughts and distractions, and we create an opportunity to be fully present in the moment. By incorporating mindfulness into our exercise routines, we can deepen the benefits of both physical activity and mindfulness, and gain a greater sense of well-being.

There are many ways to incorporate mindfulness into exercise. Here are a few of the most popular:

– Mindful Movement: This approach involves being fully present and aware of your body as you move. Focus on the sensations in your muscles, your breath, and the movements you make. Pay attention to your body's responses, and try to stay present with each moment. This type of mindfulness can be incorporated into any type of exercise, from yoga to running to weightlifting.

– Body Scanning: Before starting your exercise routine, take a moment to scan your body and become aware of any areas of tension or discomfort. Pay attention to these sensations as you move, and try to release them through the movements you make. This can be a powerful way to reduce stress and increase mindfulness.

– Mindful Breathing: Incorporating mindful breathing into your exercise routine can help you to stay present and focused. Pay attention to your breath as you move, and try to keep it slow and deep. If your mind starts to wander, simply bring your focus back to your breath. This can be particularly helpful when practicing yoga or other forms of exercise that require a lot of focus and concentration.

Exercise is a great way to cultivate mindfulness, and incorporating mindfulness into your exercise routine can help you to gain greater benefits from both. Whether you prefer yoga, running, weightlifting, or any other type of physical activity, incorporating mindfulness can help you to become more present, focused, and peaceful.

It's important to note that mindfulness should not be a replacement for seeking medical advice or professional help when it comes to physical health and wellness. Always consult with a doctor or a medical professional before starting a new exercise routine, especially if you have any medical conditions or concerns.

30: Mindfulness and Mindful Parenting

Parenting can be a challenging and rewarding experience, but it can also be stressful and overwhelming. Many parents struggle to balance their work, home, and family life, leaving little time for self-care. This is where mindfulness comes in, providing parents with a tool to manage stress, increase emotional intelligence, and cultivate a deeper connection with their children.

The practice of mindfulness helps parents stay present and aware in each moment, reducing feelings of anxiety and improving overall well-being. When parents are mindful, they are better equipped to handle difficult situations and maintain a positive outlook, which can have a significant impact on their children.

Incorporating mindfulness into parenting can be as simple as taking a few deep breaths, paying attention to your thoughts and emotions, or simply being present in the moment. These small practices can have a big impact on your relationship with your children and improve your ability to parent in a mindful and intentional way.

30: MINDFULNESS AND MINDFUL PARENTING

One effective way to incorporate mindfulness into parenting is through mindfulness exercises with your children. This can include guided meditation, deep breathing exercises, or simply taking a walk in nature and paying attention to your surroundings.

Another way to practice mindfulness as a parent is by being present during activities with your children, such as playing a game or reading a book together. By giving your full attention and being present in the moment, you model mindfulness for your children and create a stronger bond with them.

Incorporating mindfulness into your parenting practice can also help you become more aware of your own triggers and emotional responses, allowing you to respond to your children in a more mindful and intentional way. This can lead to a reduction in conflicts, improved communication, and a deeper connection with your children.

In conclusion, mindfulness and mindful parenting go hand in hand. By incorporating mindfulness into your parenting practice, you can increase your well-being, improve your relationships with your children, and model a healthy and mindful lifestyle for them to emulate. Start small and make mindfulness a part of your daily routine, and soon you will begin to see the benefits in your relationships with your children and in your own life.

31: Mindfulness and Mindful Leadership

Leadership is a critical aspect of organizational success, and it requires the ability to influence, motivate, and inspire others. As such, leaders must be able to manage their emotions, thoughts, and behaviors effectively. Mindfulness can play a crucial role in enhancing leaders' emotional intelligence, which can contribute to better relationships, communication, and decision-making skills.

The practice of mindfulness can help leaders cultivate self-awareness, which is essential for effective leadership. When leaders are aware of their thoughts, feelings, and behaviors, they can respond in a way that aligns with their values and goals. Furthermore, mindfulness enables leaders to be present in the moment, which allows them to be more attentive and responsive to others.

Mindfulness can also help leaders manage stress, which is a common challenge in high-pressure environments. Leaders who are stressed tend to make poor decisions, struggle with relationships, and have a negative impact on their teams. Mindfulness practices, such as meditation and deep breathing, can reduce stress levels and improve leaders' overall well-being.

In addition to reducing stress, mindfulness can also enhance leaders' creativity and innovation. Leaders who are mindful are more likely to have new ideas, perspectives, and approaches to challenges. Furthermore, mindfulness can help leaders become more resilient, which is essential for success in any industry.

Another critical aspect of leadership is communication. Mindful communication involves being fully present and attentive to others, and avoiding distractions, assumptions, and judgment. Mindful leaders are better equipped to listen to others and communicate effectively, which can result in better relationships and stronger teams.

In conclusion, mindfulness is a valuable tool for leaders who are looking to enhance their emotional intelligence, manage stress, improve relationships, and communicate effectively. The practice of mindfulness can provide leaders with the skills and perspective necessary to navigate challenges and lead their organizations to success.

32: Mindfulness and Mindful Entrepreneurship

As an entrepreneur, you are constantly facing challenges, making important decisions, and leading a team. Mindfulness practices can help you to remain focused, calm, and centered even in the most stressful situations. The principles of mindfulness can also help you to become a better leader, create a more positive workplace culture, and make better decisions that positively impact your business.

The practice of mindfulness can help you to become more self-aware, increase your emotional intelligence, and better understand the motivations of your employees, customers, and partners. This can lead to better relationships, increased collaboration, and improved communication.

Mindfulness can also help you to be more creative and innovative. By practicing mindfulness, you can clear your mind, reduce stress and anxiety, and open yourself up to new ideas and opportunities. Mindfulness also helps you to focus your attention on the present moment and avoid distractions, allowing you to be more productive and efficient.

Mindful entrepreneurship also involves being conscious of

the impact your business has on society and the environment. By incorporating mindfulness into your business practices, you can make ethical and sustainable decisions that are good for both your business and the world around you.

Incorporating mindfulness into your daily routine as an entrepreneur can also help you to maintain a healthy work-life balance and avoid burnout. Mindfulness can help you to stay focused and energized, even during long hours and demanding work schedules.

In conclusion, incorporating mindfulness into your entrepreneurial journey can bring numerous benefits to both you and your business. Whether you are just starting out or leading a thriving company, mindfulness can help you to become a better leader, make better decisions, and live a more fulfilling life.

33: Mindfulness and Mindful Education

The integration of mindfulness into education has been growing in recent years, with many educators recognizing the importance of teaching students how to manage their emotions, focus their attention, and develop compassion and empathy. Mindfulness can be particularly beneficial for students who struggle with anxiety, stress, or emotional regulation, helping them develop skills that can support them both inside and outside the classroom.

The benefits of mindfulness in education extend to the classroom setting itself, as well. Incorporating mindfulness practices into lessons can improve students' focus, memory retention, and ability to problem-solve. Furthermore, a mindful classroom can foster a positive and supportive learning environment, promoting teamwork and collaboration among students.

Incorporating mindfulness into education can be done in a variety of ways, such as teaching deep breathing exercises, meditation, or yoga. Educators can also incorporate mindfulness into daily routines, such as encouraging students to pause and reflect on their emotions and thoughts before starting a lesson.

Another way mindfulness can be integrated into education is through the teaching of mindfulness-based life skills, such as emotional intelligence, self-awareness, and empathy. By fostering these skills, students can learn to communicate more effectively, manage conflicts more peacefully, and build stronger relationships with peers, teachers, and family members.

In addition to the benefits for students, mindfulness can also have a positive impact on educators. By practicing mindfulness, teachers can reduce stress and improve their overall well-being, which can in turn lead to increased job satisfaction and better relationships with students.

Overall, mindfulness has the potential to positively impact the education system by promoting a supportive learning environment, improving students' emotional regulation, and fostering the development of life skills that can support students throughout their lives. By embracing the power of mindfulness in education, we can help prepare students for a successful and fulfilling future.

34: Mindfulness and Mindful Travel

Traveling can be a wonderful experience, but it can also be stressful and overwhelming. From navigating unfamiliar environments to dealing with jet lag, travel can disrupt our routines and leave us feeling out of sorts. However, with mindfulness, we can transform travel into a truly enriching experience.

The concept of mindful travel involves being fully present in the moment and enjoying each experience to the fullest. This means being aware of our thoughts and emotions, and using them to connect more deeply with the world around us. By practicing mindfulness while traveling, we can reduce stress, increase our sense of well-being, and gain a deeper appreciation for the beauty and diversity of our world.

One way to incorporate mindfulness into travel is through simple practices like paying attention to our breathing while waiting in line at an airport, or taking a few moments to observe and appreciate our surroundings while on a walk. These small acts can help us stay centered and calm, and they can make a big difference in our overall travel experience.

Mindful travel also means being fully present and engaged in each experience, whether it's trying a new food, interacting with local people, or exploring a new place. By focusing on the present moment, we can avoid getting caught up in worries about the future or regrets about the past, and instead fully immerse ourselves in the experience at hand.

In addition to individual practices, traveling with a group that focuses on mindfulness can also be a powerful experience. For example, traveling with a yoga or meditation retreat can help us stay focused and grounded, and it can provide us with opportunities to connect with like-minded people from all over the world.

Overall, incorporating mindfulness into our travel experiences can lead to greater satisfaction and a deeper appreciation for the world around us. Whether we're traveling for work or for pleasure, taking the time to be mindful can help us make the most of each experience, and create lasting memories that will stay with us for a lifetime.

35: Mindfulness and Mindful Technology

In today's fast-paced world, technology has become an integral part of our daily lives. We use technology for communication, entertainment, work, and even for relaxation. However, technology has also led to increased stress, distraction, and a lack of focus. It is important to understand how to use technology mindfully and to incorporate it into our mindfulness practices.

The practice of mindfulness can help us navigate the challenges posed by technology and the digital age. It can help us to be present in the moment, to be more aware of our thoughts and emotions, and to be less distracted by our devices. By incorporating mindfulness into our technology use, we can enhance our well-being and productivity, while avoiding the negative effects of excessive technology use.

Here are some tips for incorporating mindfulness into your technology use:

– Limit screen time: Set aside specific times for technology use, and limit your overall screen time each day. This will help you to be more present in the moment, and to focus on the things that are important to you.

– Be mindful when using your devices: When using technology, take the time to be present in the moment. Pay attention to your thoughts, emotions, and physical sensations, and try to stay focused on what you are doing.

– Turn off notifications: Turn off notifications on your devices, or limit them to specific times of the day. This will help you to avoid distractions and to be more focused when using technology.

– Incorporate technology into your mindfulness practice: There are many mindfulness apps and tools that can help you to incorporate mindfulness into your technology use. Try using guided meditations, mindfulness exercises, and mindfulness reminders, to help you stay focused and present.

– Disconnect regularly: Make sure to disconnect from technology regularly, and to spend time in nature, practicing mindfulness, or engaging in other activities that help you to recharge and relax.

In conclusion, incorporating mindfulness into our technology use is an important part of modern life. By being mindful of our technology use, we can enhance our well-being, increase our productivity, and avoid the negative effects of excessive technology use. Remember to limit screen time, be mindful when using devices, turn off notifications, incorporate technology into your mindfulness practice, and disconnect regularly.

36: Mindfulness and Mindful Aging

As we grow older, our thoughts and perspectives can change. The challenges of aging, such as physical and mental decline, loss of loved ones, and financial insecurity, can create stress and anxiety. However, mindfulness can help us navigate these challenges and experience a more peaceful and fulfilling aging process.

One of the key benefits of mindfulness is the ability to cultivate a greater sense of gratitude and appreciation for the present moment. This can help us focus on the good things in life, rather than dwelling on what we have lost or what may never be. By practicing mindfulness, we can also cultivate a deeper sense of self-awareness, which can help us understand our thoughts, feelings, and behaviors, and make changes that promote well-being.

Mindfulness can also help us improve our physical health. Research has shown that mindfulness can help reduce stress, lower blood pressure, improve sleep, and boost immune function. This is because mindfulness can help us relax, reduce muscle tension, and improve circulation. Additionally, mindfulness can help us reduce chronic pain and improve our overall sense of well-being.

Moreover, mindfulness can help us manage our emotional health. By practicing mindfulness, we can learn to become more aware of our emotions, and to respond to them in a more healthy and effective way. This can help us avoid becoming overwhelmed by negative emotions, and instead find ways to manage stress, anxiety, and depression.

Finally, mindfulness can help us cultivate a greater sense of compassion and empathy, which can improve our relationships with others. By becoming more mindful of our thoughts, feelings, and behaviors, we can become more self-aware, and better understand the thoughts, feelings, and behaviors of others. This can help us develop better relationships, and improve our ability to communicate, cooperate, and resolve conflicts.

In conclusion, mindfulness is a powerful tool that can help us navigate the challenges of aging, and improve our physical, mental, and emotional health. By practicing mindfulness, we can cultivate a greater sense of gratitude, self-awareness, compassion, and well-being, and live a more fulfilling life.

Thank You

As we reach the end of this book, I want to say thanks for reading this book.

I want to get this information out to as many people as possible. If you found this book helpful, I would greatly appreciate you leaving me a review. This helps others find the book as well.

Disclaimer

This document is geared towards providing exact and reliable information in regards to the topic and issue covered. The publication is sold on the idea that the publisher is not required to render an accounting, officially permitted, or otherwise, qualified services. If advice is necessary, legal, financial, medical or professional, a practiced individual in the profession should be ordered.

This information is not presented by a financial or medical practitioner and is for entertainment, educational and informational purposes only. The content is not intended as a substitute for professional medical advice, diagnosis, or treatment. Always seek the advice of your physician or other qualified health care provider with any questions you may have regarding a medical condition. Never disregard professional medical advice or delay in seeking it because of something you have read.

The information provided herein is stated to be truthful and consistent, in that any liability, in terms of inattention or otherwise, by any usage or abuse of any policies, processes, or directions contained within is the solitary and utter responsibility of the recipient reader. Under no circumstances

DISCLAIMER

will any legal responsibility or blame be held against the publisher for any reparation, damages, or monetary loss due to the information herein, either directly or indirectly.

www.ingramcontent.com/pod-product-compliance
Lightning Source LLC
Chambersburg PA
CBHW060339130626
46553CB00003B/1055